THE GEOGRAPHY DETECTIVE INVESTIGATES

Maps and Map Skills

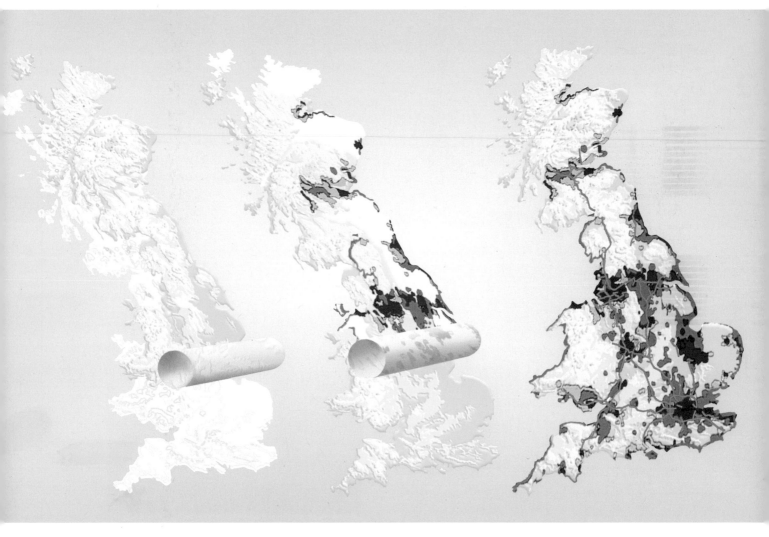

Jen Green

WAYLAND

First published in 2011 by Wayland

Copyright © Wayland 2011

Wayland
338 Euston Road
London NW1 3BH

Wayland Australia
Level 17/207 Kent Street
Sydney, NSW 2000

Senior editor: Debbie Foy
Designer: Stephen Prosser
Consultants: Jack and Meg Gillett
Picture researcher: Shelley Noronha
Artwork: Catherine Ward
Proofreader & indexer: Sarah Doughty

Picture Acknowledgements:

Cover image © Pauline St. Denis/Corbis

P4 C0037446 Library of Congress Geography
and Map Division/Science; P6l © Skyscan/Corbis;
P6r Durham/Skyscan co.uk/Imagery ©
Getmapping pic; P10 Ravenscar/Reproduced by
permission of Ordnance Survey on behalf of
HMSO © Crown copyright 2010. All rights
reserved. Ordnance Survey Licence number
0100031673; P13 Abingdon/Reproduced by
permission of Ordnance Survey on behalf of
HMSO © Crown copyright 2010. All rights
reserved. Ordnance Survey Licence number
0100031673; P15 Martindale
Common/Reproduced by permission of
Ordnance Survey on behalf of HMSO © Crown
copyright 2010. All rights reserved. Ordnance
Survey Licence number 0100031673; P16t
Huddersfield A-Z Reproduced by permission of
Geographers' A-Z Map Co Ltd. Licence No.
B5050 ©Crown Copyright 2010. All rights
reserved. Licence number 100017302; P17
Manchester Metrolink system © GMPTE; P18
Mappa Mundi/Reproduced by kind permission of
the Dean and Chapter of Hereford from the
Folio Society digitally restored reproduction of
the map; P19 AKG-images / British Library; P28
Martindale Common/Reproduced by permission

of Ordnance Survey on behalf of HMSO © Crown
copyright 2010. All rights reserved. Ordnance
Survey Licence number 0100031673; P29
Martindale Common/Reproduced by permission of
Ordnance Survey on behalf of HMSO.© Crown
copyright 2010. All rights reserved. Ordnance
Survey Licence number 0100031673; All other
illustrations © Wayland.

British Library Cataloguing in Publication Data.
Green, Jen.
    Maps and map skills. -- (The geography detective
    investigates)
    1. Maps--Juvenile literature. 2. Map reading--
    Juvenile literature.
    I. Title II. Series
    912-dc22

ISBN: 978 0 7502 6263 7

Printed in China

Wayland is a division of Hachette Children's Books,
an Hachette UK company

www.hachette.co.uk

Contents

Words that appear in **bold** can be found in the glossary on page 30.

🐾 The Geography Detective, Sherlock Bones, will help you learn all about maps and map skills. The answers to Sherlock's questions can be found on page 31.

What are maps?

Maps are drawings of the landscape viewed from high above the ground, like the view from a plane or satellite. This is called an **aerial view**. The first maps were made thousands of years ago. Cartography is the process of map-making, and people who make maps are cartographers.

Maps are incredibly useful. They help us find our way and plan journeys, whether travelling on foot or by road. Motorists, sailors and airline pilots all use maps to find their way. Town planners and architects use detailed maps called **plans**. Maps can provide lots of different kinds of information about an area. Learning to read a map is an important skill. This book will take you through it step by step.

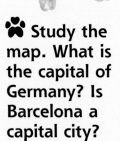

✿ **Study the map. What is the capital of Germany? Is Barcelona a capital city?**

This political map of Western Europe shows its major cities as black dots, and its capital cities (shown in bold) as stars.

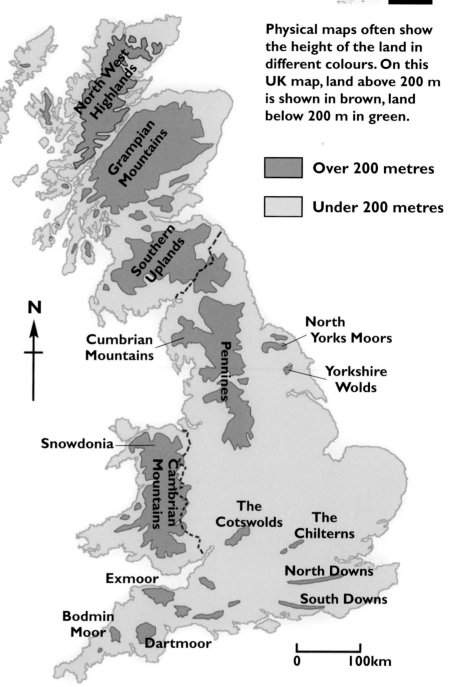

Atlases

An atlas is a book of maps. The name comes from Atlas, a giant in Greek mythology who supported the world on his powerful shoulders. The term was first used to describe a book of maps in the 1500s by the great Flemish map-maker, Gerardus Mercator (1512-1594).

There are many different kinds of maps. Some atlas maps show a very large area such as a country or even the whole world. Street maps show a much smaller area, like a city centre.

Many maps use colour to convey information. Physical maps present the **topography**, or lie of the land, with natural features such as mountains and rivers. Lowlands are often displayed in green, high ground in brown, and the highest mountains in white and purple.

Political maps show the borders of countries, states and provinces. Countries are often displayed in different colours to make it easier to see their outlines. General maps show both natural features such as rivers, and man-made features such as roads.

Physical maps often show the height of the land in different colours. On this UK map, land above 200 m is shown in brown, land below 200 m in green.

Over 200 metres

Under 200 metres

North West Highlands

Grampian Mountains

Southern Uplands

N

Cumbrian Mountains

North Yorks Moors

Pennines

Yorkshire Wolds

Snowdonia

Cambrian Mountains

The Cotswolds

The Chilterns

North Downs

South Downs

Exmoor

Bodmin Moor

Dartmoor

0   100km

DETECTIVE WORK

Maps are made from a high viewpoint above the ground. Try making a map of your street from a top-floor window, or draw the centre of town looking out of the window of a tall building. Compare your map with a local map. If you were able to get high above the landscape your map may be quite accurate.

Why do maps use symbols?

Maps are rather like aerial photographs. However unlike aerial photos, which show everything visible from the air, maps often leave many things out to make them less cluttered. Maps give a simplified view of the landscape so that the most important features stand out. They don't show moving features such as cars and people.

Maps use **symbols** (signs) to represent hills, rivers, lakes, buildings, and other features. You may already know the map symbols for roads, woodlands, lakes and buildings such as churches. All symbols shown on the map appear in the **key**, usually provided next to the map. Before using a map, study the key to make sure you understand the symbols. It's easy to confuse certain symbols, such as boundaries and footpaths.

This aerial photo of the city of Durham was taken by an aircraft with a camera pointing at an angle. This is called an **oblique viewpoint**.

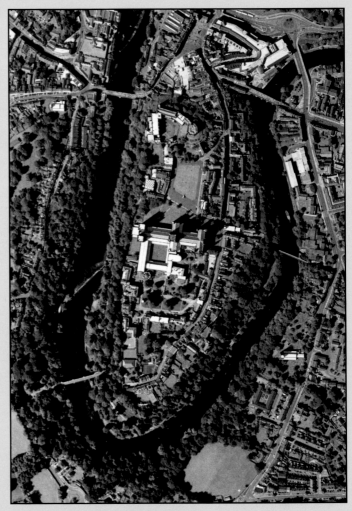

This aerial view of Durham was taken from directly above. The exact size and position of features are shown, but they are not always easy to recognise. This is known as a bird's eye view.

Ordnance Survey

Ordnance Survey (OS for short) is the UK's main mapping organisation. This was once a military organisation, but is now a civilian government agency. The first OS maps were drawn up in the late 1790s, when Britain was at risk of invasion from France. The maps were commissioned by the Board of Ordnance, which later became the Ministry of Defence. The word 'ordnance' means weapons.

Map symbols include lines that can represent roads, streams or rivers. Symbols also include letters, which are usually an abbreviation of the word, to save space on the map. For example, the letters PO stand for post office, Lib for library and Sch for school. Some symbols are coloured areas – for example, water is shown in blue, and woodlands in green. Finally, map symbols include drawings, for example a little flag stands for a golf course, a cross stands for a church and a broad-leaved tree stands for woodland areas.

A map of Durham uses symbols to provide more information.

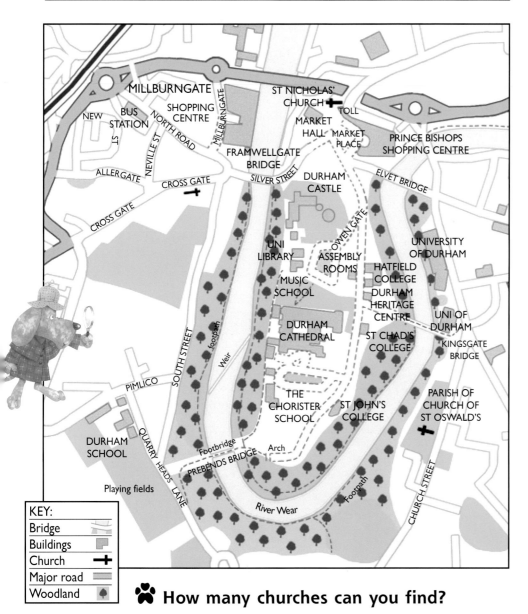

KEY:
Bridge	
Buildings	
Church	
Major road	
Woodland	

🐾 **How many churches can you find?**

DETECTIVE WORK

Check out Ordnance Survey maps online by logging onto http://mapzone. ordnancesurvey.co. uk/mapzone/info.html. You can also see a map of your area by logging onto www2.getmapping. com and typing in your postcode.

How do maps show scale and distance?

All maps are drawn to a greatly reduced **scale**. If shown anything like actual size, they would be far too large to use! The whole map is shrunk to a particular size – this is called drawing to scale. The scale is shown in the scale bar at the edge of the map. The smaller the area is drawn, the smaller the scale.

Before you use a map, you need to familiarise yourself with its scale. This will give you a sense of the size of the area shown, and an estimate of your journey time if you are travelling. Small-scale maps show a large area in not much detail. For example, on an OS 1:50,000 map, 1 cm on the map represents 50,000 cm on the ground (0.5 km). So 2 cm covers 1 km. Road maps use even smaller scales such as 1:100,000, where 1 cm on the map represents 1 km. Atlas maps are often *very* small-scale.

FOCUS ON

Estimating distance

You can estimate the length of journeys quite accurately using a piece of string and a map. Lay the string along your route, taking care to follow any curves along roads or paths. Now lay the string along the scale bar on the map as many times as necessary. On level ground, most people cover about 4 km an hour when walking briskly. Divide the number of kilometres by four to work out how long your journey will take by foot.

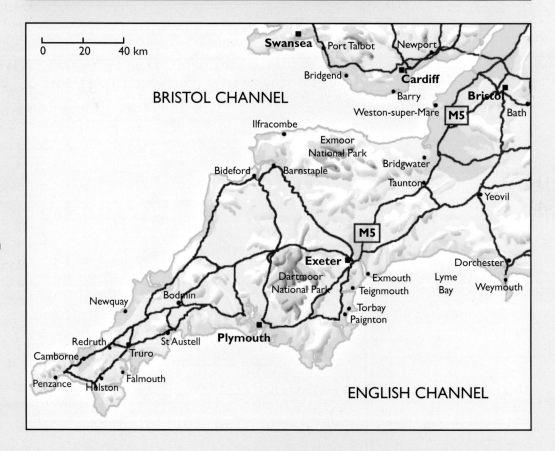

This small-scale map shows the whole of Devon and Cornwall.

This larger-scale map shows Cornwall in more detail.

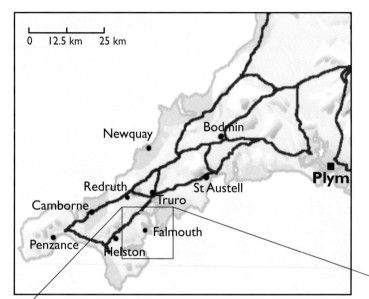

0   12.5 km   25 km

Newquay
Bodmin
Redruth
St Austell
Camborne
Truro
Plym
Penzance
Falmouth
Helston

Large-scale maps show a small area in much more detail. On an OS 1:25,000 map, 1 cm on the map represents 250 m (0.25 km) in real life. These maps are useful to walkers and cyclists who need to keep track of exactly where they are. Street maps show an area in even greater detail, giving street names, which allow you to find your way around town. Confusingly, in the UK, both imperial and metric measurements are used for distances. OS maps give distances in kilometres, while signposts use miles!

A39
Carnon Downs
A3078
Upper Tredrea
Devoran
Penpol
A393
Ponsanooth
Mylor Bridge
Portscatho
A39
A3078
Tremough
Penryn
St Mawes
A394
Kernick
Falmouth
Port Pendennis
Carrick Roads
Budock Water
Goldenbank
Swanpool
Falmouth Bay

0   2.5   5 km

This large-scale map shows Falmouth Bay and its surroundings. You can see the shape of settlements and the coastline, and some road names.

🐾 **Look at the large-scale map of Falmouth Bay. Which road leads from Carnon Downs into Falmouth?**

Why do maps have grids?

Most maps have a **grid** that gives east-west distance on lines that run up and down vertically, and north-south distance on lines running horizontally (sideways). The grid is numbered or lettered, which allows you to plot co-ordinates and pinpoint locations.

On OS maps grid lines are marked in blue and numbered. Each grid square covers 1 square kilometre. Co-ordinates are plotted giving the east-west distance first, by running your finger sideways from the left-hand corner of the map. Note the two-figure number. Then plot the north-south distance by running your finger upwards and note that number. Remember this order with the phrase 'along the corridor and up the stairs'. The numbers provide a four-figure **grid reference**. On the map shown below, Beacon Windmill is in square 9700. You can make a more accurate six-figure reference by estimating the number of tenths across and then up the grid square. For example the six-figure grid reference for Beacon Windmill is 976006.

DETECTIVE WORK

What is the total area shown on the map? Estimate how long it would take you to walk from the car park in the centre of Ravenscar to Danesdale in square 9800 via the path that leads off Bent Rigg Lane.

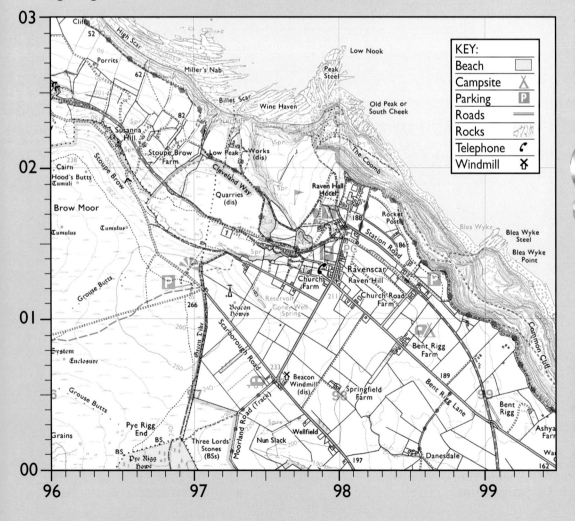

This 1:25,000 OS map shows the village of Ravenscar in North Yorkshire.

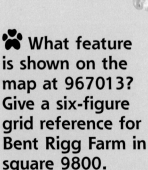

What feature is shown on the map at 967013? Give a six-figure grid reference for Bent Rigg Farm in square 9800.

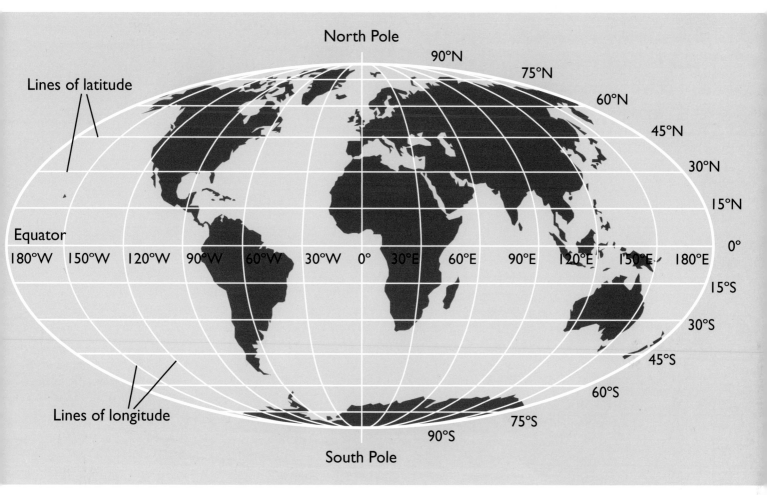

North Pole
90°N
75°N
60°N
45°N
30°N
15°N
0°
15°S
30°S
45°S
60°S
75°S
90°S
South Pole

Lines of latitude

Lines of longitude

Equator
180°W 150°W 120°W 90°W 60°W 30°W 0° 30°E 60°E 90°E 120°E 150°E 180°E

Lines of latitude all run parallel to the Equator.
Lines of longitude meet at the North and South Poles.

The grid lines on an OS map allow you to estimate the length of journeys. Counting the number of squares your route passes through gives you the rough distance in kilometres. If you walk at 4 km per hour it will take you about 15 minutes to cross each square.

The grid lines on OS maps are part of a huge grid covering the whole world. These lines are called **latitude** and **longitude**. Lines of latitude, known as parallels, measure the distance north or south of the Equator. All latitudes above the Equator have the letter N after them. For example, London lies at about 51°N. Lines of longitude, known as meridians, measure east-west distance. Longitude 0, known as the Prime Meridian, passes though Greenwich in London.

FOCUS ON

Navigating at sea

By 1600 AD, sailors were able to calculate latitude at sea by observing the height of the sun at midday. Longitude was much more difficult to calculate. It depended on inventing an accurate clock that could be used at sea. In the 1770s, English clockmaker John Harrison devised an accurate sea clock.

How do maps show direction?

All maps are aligned to a particular compass direction. Most but not all maps show north at the top. The north arrow will be shown near the key. A compass is a vital tool in navigation.

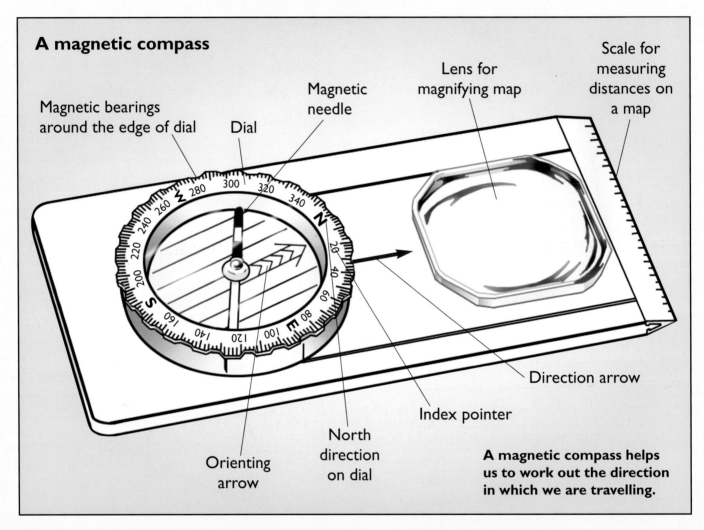

A magnetic compass

Magnetic bearings around the edge of dial

Dial

Magnetic needle

Lens for magnifying map

Scale for measuring distances on a map

Direction arrow

Index pointer

North direction on dial

Orienting arrow

A magnetic compass helps us to work out the direction in which we are travelling.

Understanding how to use a compass can help you find your way even without a map. The four main points of the compass: north, south, east and west, are arranged around the dial in a 360° circle. The red floating compass needle always points to magnetic north. If you know you need to head, say, generally east, use your compass to find where north lies. East lies to the right of it, at a right-angle (90°). The points of the compass also allow you to describe the location of places. For example, on the map on the opposite page, Craighead Hill lies northwest of Abington. Crawford lies southeast of Abington.

DETECTIVE WORK

Make a basic compass using a needle, magnet, round slice of cork and a bowl of water. Magnetise the needle by stroking it with the magnet, about 50 times in the same direction. Balance the needle on the slice of cork and float it in the water. The needle will turn to point north.

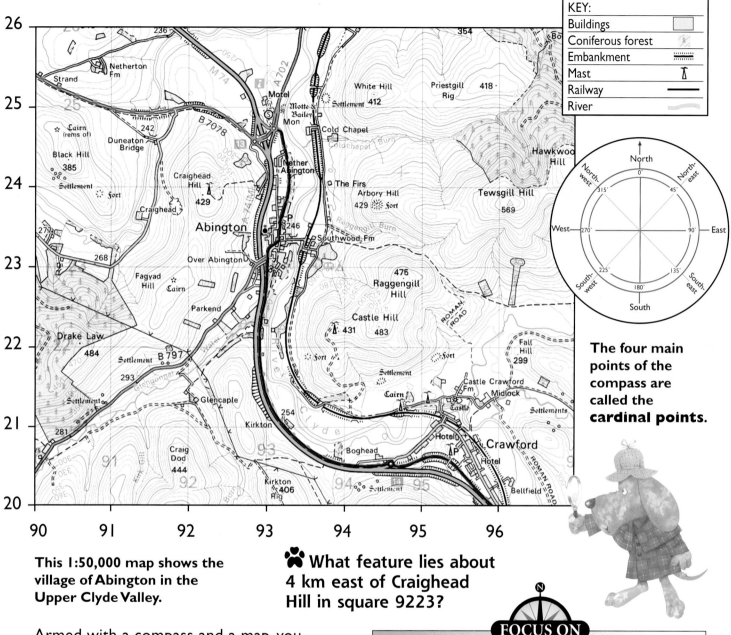

KEY:
Buildings	
Coniferous forest	
Embankment	
Mast	
Railway	
River	

The four main points of the compass are called the cardinal points.

This 1:50,000 map shows the village of Abington in the Upper Clyde Valley.

🐾 **What feature lies about 4 km east of Craighead Hill in square 9223?**

Armed with a compass and a map, you can travel confidently through unknown territory! Finding out how north on the map relates to north on the ground is called setting the map. Place the long edge of your compass along the map in the direction you want to travel. Turn the inner dial so it points to north on the map. Now take the compass off the map and turn around until the magnetic needle points north. The direction arrow outside the dial shows your direction. Off you go!

FOCUS ON

History of compasses

Compasses have been used for centuries. They were certainly in use in China by the thirteenth century AD, and probably a lot earlier. Experts believe the invention spread west along the trade route called the Silk Road. By the thirteenth century European and Arab sailors were using compasses.

What are contour lines?

Map-makers have always found it difficult to show the ups and downs of the landscape on the flat surface of a map. Some maps get around this using shading or by drawing little pictures of mountains. But on most maps lines called **contour lines** are used to show **relief** – the height of the land.

Contour lines join places at the same height above sea level. On a 1:50,000 map each contour line represents 10 m. Every 5 lines or 50 m is shown by a darker line. On a 1:25,000 map each line represents 5 metres. Figures called **spot heights** give the heights of particular points such as a **summit**. The height numbers are always printed looking uphill so you can tell which way the land is sloping.

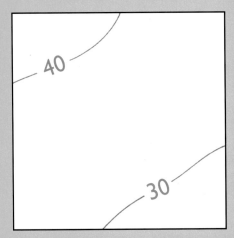

Contours are widely spaced on gentle slopes.

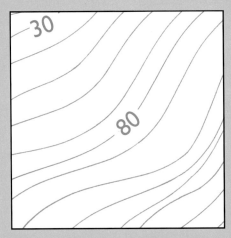

On steep slopes they are close together.

This shows an area of high land such as a mountain.

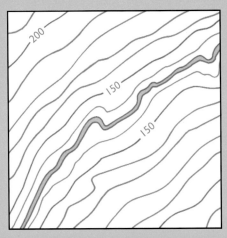

This shows a steep valley with a river flowing through it.

FOCUS ON

Timing uphill journeys

Going uphill always takes longer than walking over flat ground. Not only does climbing take more effort, but you are also covering extra ground that cannot be shown on a flat map! You need to take this into account when estimating journey times when walking in hill country. Use the contour lines to work out your total height gain, by subtracting the starting height of each climb from the summit height. Add an extra half hour for each 300 m you climb. Downhill stretches count the same as walking on the flat.

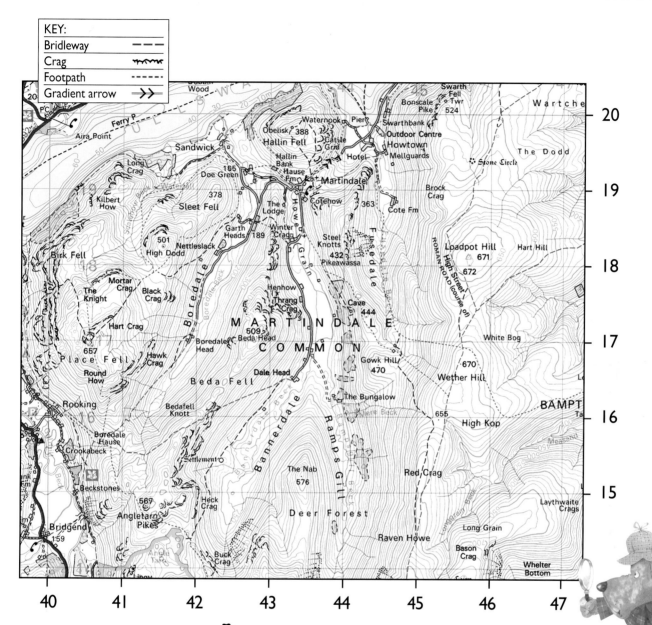

KEY:
Bridleway	– – –
Crag	ᐷᐷᐷ
Footpath	··········
Gradient arrow	⟩⟩

This 1:50,000 OS map shows Martindale Common in the English Lake District.

🐾 **In what type of landscape is the village of Martindale located? What is the terrain like between Martindale and Howtown to the northeast?**

Looking closely at contour lines allows you to identify features such as hills, mountains, ridges, cliffs and valleys. If the contour lines are shown close together the slope is steep. If they are spaced out the land slopes gently. Where they are practically on top of one another, there is a cliff. Cliffs and crags are also marked with special symbols. On steep roads the **gradient** (slope) is marked with gradient arrows (>>), pointing downhill.

DETECTIVE WORK

Estimate the time it would take you to walk from Garth Heads in square 4218 southwest to the top of High Dodd.

How are maps useful on journeys?

One of the main uses of maps is to plan and make journeys. Different types and scales of map are most useful when travelling on foot, or by car, bus and train.

Large-scale OS maps are ideal for walkers, cyclists and horse-riders. OS maps have different symbols for footpaths which are for walkers only, for bridleways which are used by cyclists and horse-riders. Street maps show city centres in a lot of detail, naming every road and marking one-way systems and pedestrian areas. Road maps show a large area in much less detail, so they are useful for long journeys. Major roads and motorways are coloured differently and numbered. The map only contains the information needed to get you from one place to another.

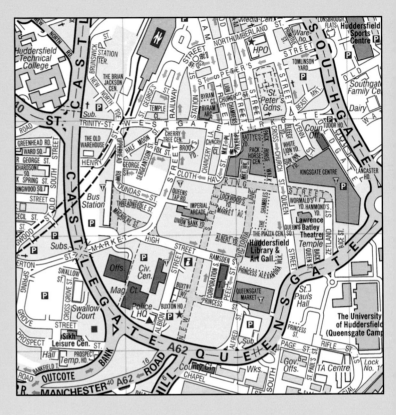

This street map of Huddersfield, Yorkshire, gives street names and information for motorists, such as one-way streets and car parks.

A road atlas map showing the routes between Birmingham and Liverpool.

Key
— Motorway
— Primary route
• Town or city

DETECTIVE WORK

Make a map of your journey to school, from memory. Write in all the street names you know, and any landmarks that help you find your way. Compare your map to a local street map. Is your memory map geographically accurate? Does it matter if it isn't?

FOCUS ON

London Underground

The famous London Underground map was designed in the 1930s by an underground employee, Harry Beck. Beck realised that since most of the network lay underground, it was not important to show the precise location of stations, merely their relation to one another. Underground lines and the River Thames appear as straight lines. The central area is enlarged so it is clearer. Beck was paid just over £5 for his amazing map!

Schematic maps, called topological maps, look very different to ordinary maps. This map of the Manchester Metro is a good example.

OS, street and road maps show locations accurately because we need that information for navigation. Transport maps such as bus and train maps don't need to be accurate in this way. They leave out a lot of detail and only show the connections between stations, so we know where to get off or change buses or trains.

✿ **Study the Manchester Metrolink map. What is the quickest way of getting from Ladywell, near the end of the Eccles Line, to Navigation Road near the southern end of the Bury / Altrincham Line?**

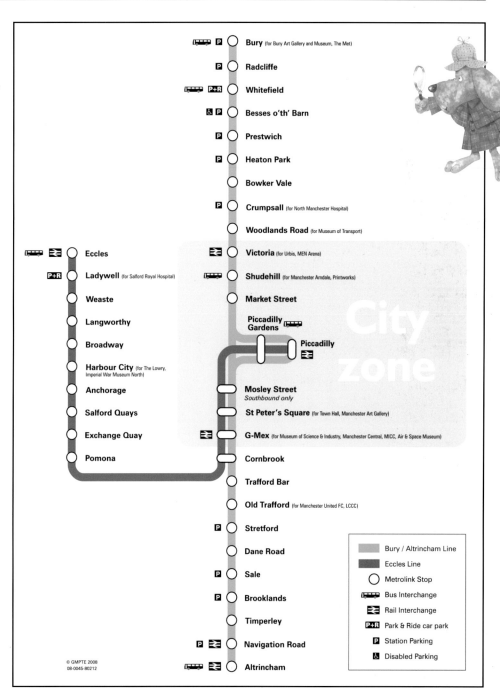

What were early maps like?

Maps are among the earliest human records. The oldest surviving map is over 4,000 years old. Etched into a clay tablet found in Iraq, it shows hills, streams and villages. Maps were also made in ancient Egypt and China, on silk, stone or papyrus. The ancient Greeks were skilled geographers. Around 150 AD the Greek scholar Ptolemy of Alexandria compiled a series of eight books on geography. It included a world map and 26 regional maps. Ptolemy used the terms latitude and longitude and offered advice on how to display Earth's curving surface onto a flat map.

FOCUS ON

Cassini's maps of France

In the late 1600s, the great French map-maker Jacques Cassini used a technique called **triangulation** to calculate the distances between locations. Cassini had the grand plan of mapping all of France, but did not live to see the project completed. The last of 182 maps were completed over 100 years later by his great-grandson.

The Hereford Mappa Mundi is housed at Hereford Cathedral and was drawn about 1300 AD. It is a T and O map (see below), with the holy city of Jerusalem at the centre of the known world.

Later, much Greek and Roman knowledge of geography was lost. In medieval times Arabs were the most advanced map-makers. European maps of the time are called T and O maps because they show the known world arranged around a T-shaped sea and surrounded by a circle of ocean. From the mid-1400s, the invention of printing made maps cheaper and more common. Of course, all maps can only reflect the knowledge of their time. Before 1500 European maps did not show the Americas, Australia or Antarctica. In the late 1400s, the discovery of the New World by Christopher Columbus led to a surge of interest in map-making.

By the 1600s map-making was a small but important industry. The information was gathered by teams of **surveyors** who measured heights and distances on the ground. In the late 1600s, maps became more accurate due to a new method of calculating distance called triangulation. In the 1780s, the invention of the hot-air balloon made it possible to see the Earth's surface from the air for the first time. In the 1900s, the invention of aircraft and then satellites revolutionised map-making.

DETECTIVE WORK

Find a modern map of London and compare it with the historic map shown here. What features are the same? What new transport networks make it easier to get about?

This early map of London from 1845 shows certain landmarks that are still familiar today.

☙ **How many bridges can you see on this map?**

How are modern maps made?

In days gone by, map-making was a slow, painstaking process involving huge amounts of time and energy. Surveyors spent hundreds of hours collecting data by making precise measurements. In 1819, the Director-General of the Ordnance Survey walked 586 miles in 22 days during a survey! Nowadays a lot of this work is carried out by automatic sensors and computers.

Computer systems called Geographic Information Systems (GIS) are central to modern map-making. These systems include a computer, software and a database holding huge amounts of information, often gathered by **remote sensing** equipment.

When cartographers begin work on a map, the first step is always to gather data. Some of this work is still done by surveying teams on the ground, but most is done by automated cameras mounted on aircraft and satellites. The information is stored on a database. Data on landforms, settlements, road networks and urban areas is stored in separate 'layers'. This allows map-makers to select certain strands of data depending on the purpose of the map.

DETECTIVE WORK

Interactive programmes such as GoogleEarth allow you to zoom in and out to change the scale of any map. You can also select different perspectives, viewing Earth's surface from either directly overhead or from an oblique angle. Try using GoogleEarth on a computer at home, school or in a library.

1. A relief map is built up

2. Main settlements are added

3. The final map is packed with information, including motorway links.

Modern maps are built up by superimposing several layers of data from a GIS database.

Once the map's purpose is agreed, the cartographer selects data and also decides on the scale and design, including the symbols and colours that will show the information most clearly. When the map has been perfected on screen and checked thoroughly, it is published. Later it can be revised using new information.

Some maps are designed mainly to be seen on a computer screen, though viewers are usually able to print them if they choose. The data may be stored on a CD-Rom or available on the Internet. Interactive programmes such as GoogleEarth allow viewers to make their own decisions about scale and perspective.

FOCUS ON

Mapping unexplored territory

Remote sensors and GIS allow modern cartographers to make maps of regions that have never been explored on foot, such as the surface of the Moon, the icy wastes of Antarctica and even the ocean floor. Undersea terrain is mapped using **sonar**. The research ship directs a beam of sound at the ocean floor and records the time the echoes take to bounce back to the ship.

A research ship uses sonar to chart the sea floor. In the mid-1900s scientists using sonar discovered mountain chains running down the centre of the oceans, higher and longer than any on land!

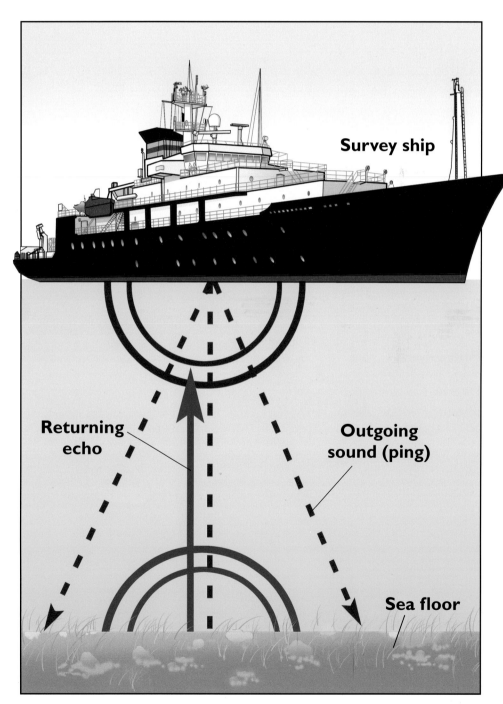

Survey ship

Returning echo

Outgoing sound (ping)

Sea floor

Why is it hard to show the Earth on a map?

The Earth is a giant rocky sphere. The only way to show its surface accurately is on a globe, where the shapes of landmasses can be drawn and positioned accurately. The drawback is that globes are expensive to produce. They are also awkward to carry about.

In contrast, maps are quite easy to produce. Maps printed on paper can be conveniently folded and are light and easy to carry. However, it is impossible to show the Earth's curving surface accurately on a flat map. Cartographers use mathematic approaches called **projections** to show the Earth on flat paper. There are over 200 different projections, but relatively few are commonly used. All projections involve some degree of distortion – some areas are flattened or compressed, while others are stretched out.

Mercator's Projection distorts the far north and south of the globe. This makes Greenland appear about the same size as Africa, whereas it is really much smaller.

Mercator's Projection

Flemish cartographer Gerardus Mercator devised his projection in 1569. It was mainly intended for marine navigation. Sailors could use the map to set their compass direction, and plot their route to any destination as a straight line. However, Mercator's Projection distorts the areas close to the Poles.

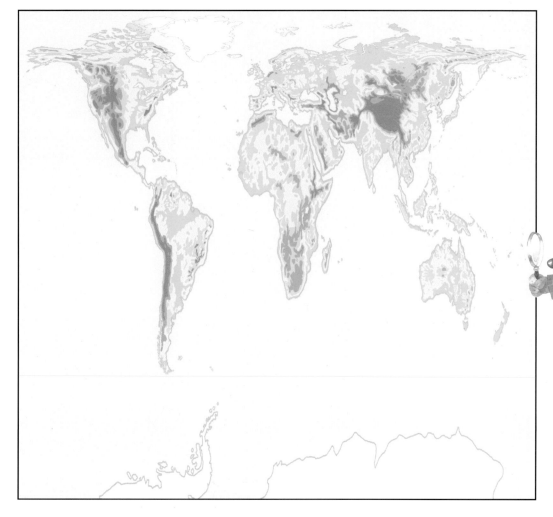

Peters' Projection stretches the continents lengthwise to show their true size.

🐾 Compare the relative sizes of Greenland and South America on the two maps.

DETECTIVE WORK

Try this experiment with projection. Use a pen to draw circles, triangles and squares on a satsuma to represent the shapes of the continents. Now carefully peel the satsuma and flatten it out. Notice what happens to the shapes you have drawn.

Mercator's Projection, invented over 400 years ago, is still commonly used. This projection shows the shapes of continents fairly accurately but distorts their size, particularly in the most northerly and southerly parts of the globe. This makes Europe look much larger than it really is. In contrast, Peters' Projection, devised in the 1970s, shows the true size of continents but stretches their shapes. Homolographic or equal-area projections show the size and shape of continents much more accurately. But they divide the globe into segments, which makes the map hard to read.

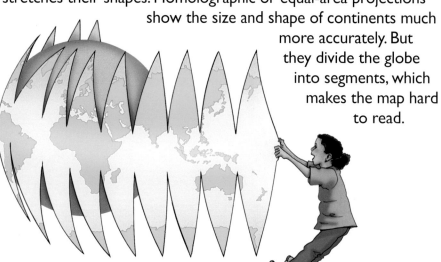

Homolographic projections divide the world into segments. The gaps in the landmasses make it hard to use these maps.

What are thematic maps?

Maps can convey all sorts of information. Some of the main uses of maps are to show natural features, national borders and transport networks, but maps can also be used to show cultural information, such as the language spoken in a region, or the main religion. Any information that relates to a particular location or country can be shown on a map.

Thematic maps show particular information, such as where people live, the type of farming, or the rocks and minerals found at the surface. Land use maps show how the land is used, whether for homes, business, industry or recreation. **Population density maps** show where people live. Climate and weather maps show features such as rainfall, temperature, wind and cloud type.

FOCUS ON

Understanding cholera

The 1850s saw an outbreak of cholera in London. This disease is caused by drinking polluted water, but no one knew this at the time. A doctor named John Snow tried to find the cause of the outbreak. When he recorded cholera deaths as dots on a map of London, he noticed that the dots clustered around a pump in Broad Street. Snow realised the polluted well was causing the outbreak.

KEY

- water pump
- cholera cases
- roads
- perimeter of cholera outbreak in London.

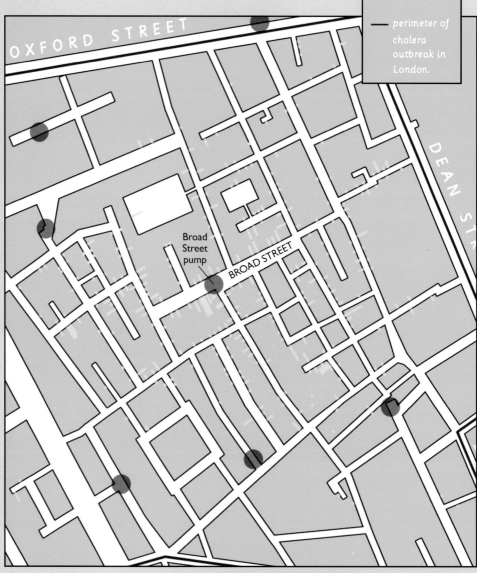

Snow's map of central London showing cholera cases.

Different styles of map are best suited for different kinds of information. **Dot maps** are useful to show population. Each dot represents a particular unit, for example 10,000 or 100,000 people. But if areas are very densely or sparsely populated, it is hard to position the dots accurately. **Choropleth maps** use colour and shading to show information such as rainfall or height above sea level. Different tones of just one or two colours are often used, with dark colours representing high values, such as heavy rainfall. Isopleth maps use lines to join places that have the same value, for example, contour lines, which join places at the same height. On weather maps, **isotherms** are lines that link places with the same temperature. **Isobars** link areas with the same air pressure.

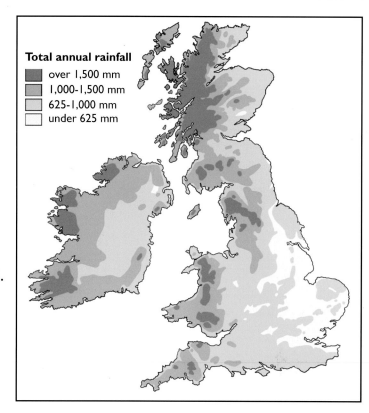

Total annual rainfall
- over 1,500 mm
- 1,000-1,500 mm
- 625-1,000 mm
- under 625 mm

This choropleth map shows rainfall distribution in the UK. The dark colour represents the region with highest rainfall.

🐾 **What parts of Britain get the highest rainfall?**

DETECTIVE WORK

Make a dot map to show how far pupils in your class travel to school. Trace or copy a local map. Put the school in the centre and mark the address of each pupil with a dot. If some pupils travel a long way you will need to make a small-scale map. If everyone lives nearby, the scale of your map can be larger.

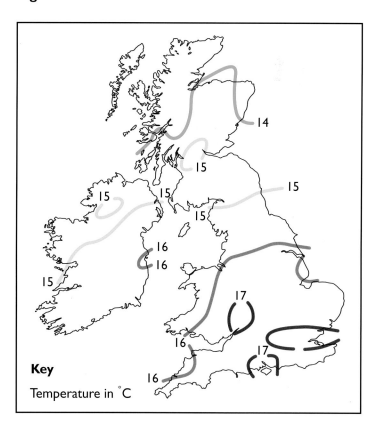

Key
Temperature in °C

This map shows average UK summer temperatures. The lines are called isotherms.

Are maps always accurate?

No map can be entirely accurate! Features such as streams and streets are too narrow to be shown actual size. Map symbols are always printed to a standard size, whatever the size of the real feature. All maps leave out certain information in the interests of keeping the map clear and simple. This is called de-cluttering.

Some maps show information that is invisible from the air or on the ground, such as tunnels, subways and country boundaries. Others make use of special imaging techniques such as **infrared** and **radar**, to show things that are invisible to the naked eye. Infrared sensors detect the warmth of land and sea surfaces or cloud cover. They can be used to show ocean temperatures or the type of vegetation. On weather maps, rainfall is detected using radar equipment that picks up radio waves bounced off rainclouds.

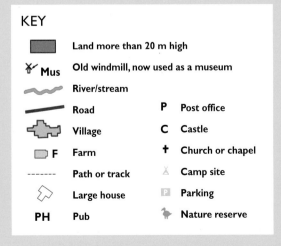

FOCUS ON

Sketch maps

Geographers use sketch maps to show selected features. Simple colours are often used to highlight the features the map-maker wants to emphasise. You could try drawing a sketch map of your local area from an OS map. Pencil in the rough shapes of rivers, roads and settlements. Colour in the features and add a key. Label the main features. Keep the map simple, but try to be reasonably accurate.

This sketch map of the village of Burwell uses colour to show the key features. A lot of detail is left out.

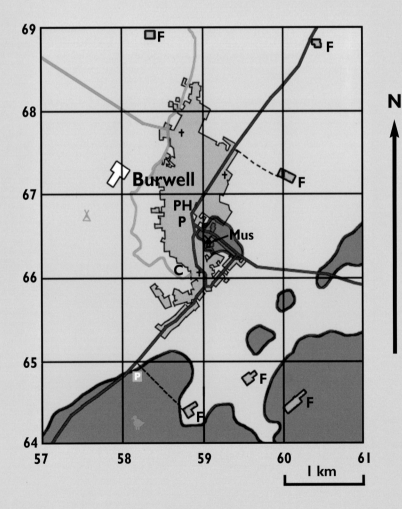

N

KEY

▬	Land more than 20 m high		
✗ Mus	Old windmill, now used as a museum		
∿	River/stream		
▬	Road	**P**	Post office
Village		**C**	Castle
▭ F	Farm	**✝**	Church or chapel
------	Path or track	⅄	Camp site
◇	Large house	P	Parking
PH	Pub		Nature reserve

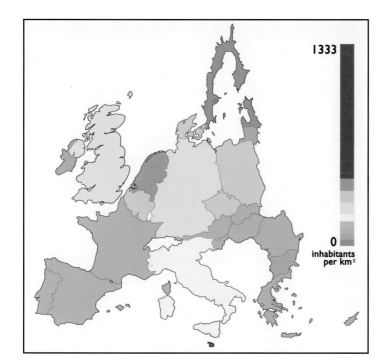

In this cartogram of the European Union, country sizes have been distorted to reflect the size of each country's population.

Some maps sacrifice geographical accuracy to provide other kinds of information. Maps called **cartograms** deliberately distort the size and shape of countries to show subjects such as population distribution more clearly. Tourist maps aren't concerned with much geographical detail. They use drawings of landmarks or activities to show what the region is most famous for. In short, maps don't necessarily have to be accurate to be useful!

Compare the cartogram with an 'ordinary' map of the same area. Which countries are the most densely populated?

Tourist maps such as this one drawn before the break up of the Soviet Union in 1991 show what different regions are most famous for.

DETECTIVE WORK

Make a tourist map of your town or local area. Trace (or copy) a map. Add drawings of landmarks and main attractions. You could add symbols for leisure facilities such as cinemas, sports grounds and swimming pools.

Your project

I f you've done the detective work throughout the book and answered all of Sherlock's questions, you will now know a lot about maps and mapping! Use this information to produce your own project on maps.

Practical mapping

• The two maps here show Martindale Common in the Lake District to different scales. Which map would you use to plan a hike? Which one would you prefer on the actual hike?

• Study the maps. What is the general terrain like – is it flat or hilly? What is the highest point shown? Where do local streams flow to? Do valleys run mainly east to west, or north to south?

• Study the map below. What features would you see at grid references 430175 and 418190? Give the six-figure grid reference for the cave in square 4417.

• You are planning a hike from Howtown south to Gowk Hill via Fusedale. From there you'll head northwest to Winter Crag and take the footpath to Garth Heads. Then you head north to Sandwick, and back to Howtown. What landscape would you expect to see on each stage of your hike?

• Estimate how long the walk will take you. Count the squares you cross or use string to measure the route (see page 8). Now study the contours. Total the height climbed on all uphill stages. Add an extra half hour for each 300 metres you climb.

• Imagine you are at the start of the walk. Set your compass for the first direction you will take. In what general direction is the final leg along the lake?

This OS map shows Martindale Common in the Lake District to a scale of 1:50,000.

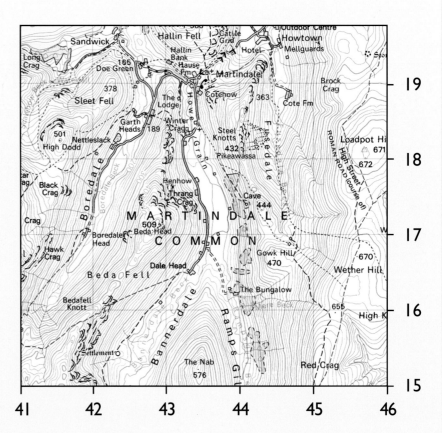

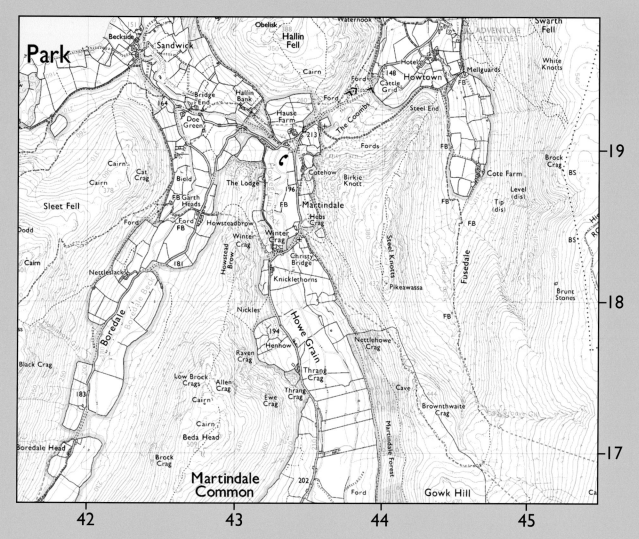

Other topics

The same area shown on the 1:25,000 map.

- Track down historic maps that show the world before and after the great age of exploration (1400-1550). Find out more about navigation at sea either in past times or today.

- Make a scale map of your classroom using the technique on page 9. Plot the basic room shape on graph paper and mark the location of doors, windows, furniture and shelves.

- Use the library or Internet to research early maps of your town or local area. Compare them with a modern map. What are the main changes you see? Think about public buildings, transport networks and the size of towns and villages.

- Find out more about mapping unexplored areas such as the Moon, the ocean floor and Antarctica. What special equipment is needed to do this? What are these maps then used for?

Your local library and the Internet can provide all sorts of information. Try the websites listed on page 31.

Glossary

Aerial view A view of the landscape from above.

Cardinal points The four main points of the compass, i.e. north, south, east and west.

Cartogram A map which distorts geographical detail in order to convey information.

Choropleth map A map that uses colour to show information.

Contour line A line on a map that joins places at a particular height above sea level.

Dot map A map that uses dots to show information.

Gradient The steepness of a slope.

Grid A network of lines, for example on a map.

Grid reference A method of pinpointing locations on maps using grid line numbers.

Infrared A form of radiation that is invisible.

Isobar A line that links areas with the same air pressure.

Isotherm A line that links places with the same temperature.

Key A display of map symbols and their meanings.

Latitude A system of lines running east-west across the globe, marking distance north or south of the Equator. Latitude lines are also called parallels and are followed by the letters N and S (north or south).

Longitude A system of lines running between the North and South Poles, marking east-west distance. Longitude lines are also called meridians and are followed by the letters W and E (west or east).

Oblique viewpoint Photograph or drawing made looking downwards at an angle.

Ordnance Survey (OS) Britain's official map-making organisation.

Plan A detailed scale map of a house, district or town.

Population density map This map shows the number of people living in a particular location.

Projection A mathematical method of showing Earth's curving surface on a flat map.

Radar Equipment used to detect objects by bouncing radio waves off them.

Relief The height and shape of the landscape.

Remote sensing Production of images using satellites.

Scale The particular size a map is drawn to.

Sonar A system used to detect underwater objects using sound waves.

Spot height The height of a particular point above sea level, given on a map.

Summit The highest point of a mountain or hill.

Surveyor A person who gathers data for maps by measuring heights and distances.

Symbol A sign or drawing on a map which represents a feature on the ground such as a church.

Terrain The type of landscape.

Thematic map A map which shows a particular type of information, such as population or climate.

Triangulation A method of calculating distances between locations using three surveying points.

Topography The ups and downs of a landscape.

Topological map A map that shows places, and the transport networks which link them.

Answers

🐾 **Page 4:** Berlin is the capital of Germany. Madrid, not Barcelona, is the capital of Spain.

🐾 **Page 7:** Three churches are shown on the map.

🐾 **Page 9:** The road leading from Carnon Downs into Falmouth is the A39.

🐾 **Page 10:** The feature is a car park; the reference is 985008.

🐾 **Page 13:** The feature is Tewsgill Hill.

🐾 **Page 15:** Martindale is located in a narrow valley between mountains. The road from Martindale climbs steeply up and then drops down into Howtown.

🐾 **Page 15:** (Answer to Detective work) The distance between Garth Heads and High Dodd is only about 1 km, which would take 15 minutes on the flat. However the height gain is 312 metres

(501 m at High Dodd minus 189 m at Garth Heads), so you need to add an extra half-hour, making the walk three-quarters of an hour.

🐾 **Page 17:** Take the Eccles Line as far as Cornbrook where you can change onto the Bury / Altrincham Line and head south to Navigation Road.

🐾 **Page 19** Six bridges are present on the map.

🐾 **Page 25:** Western parts of the UK get the most rain. These mainly mountainous areas lie in the path of moist winds blowing off the Atlantic Ocean.

🐾 **Page 27:** The cartogram shows that the Netherlands, Belgium, the UK and Germany are densely populated countries.

Further information

Further reading

Introducing Maps; Understanding Local Maps; Understanding World Maps; Using Maps, Jack and Meg Gillett (Wayland Books, 2008)

Mapping Britain's Landscapes: Hills and Mountains; Cities, Towns and Villages, Jen Green (Franklin Watts, 2007)

Mapping Settlements, Louise Spilsbury (Heinemann, 2005)

Maps and Mapping, Deborah Chancellor (Kingfisher, 2004)

Websites

Ordnance Survey Mapzone: This website offers games, advice with homework and much more: http://mapzone.ordnancesurvey.co.uk/mapzone/info.html.

Getmapping.com: Log onto this website for maps and aerial photos of the UK, including historical images: www2.getmapping.com

Google Earth: This website offers satellite imagery, maps, and 3D images of the Earth's landscape: http://earth.google.com, also http://earth.google.co.uk

Met Office UK: Look at this website for weather and climate maps of the UK: http://metoffice.org

Greenpeace UK
http://www.greenpeace.org.uk

Friends of the Earth
http://www.foe.co.uk

Worldwide Fund for Nature
http://www.wwf.org.uk

Index

The Geography Detective Investigates

Contents of titles in the series:

WAYLAND